Lora Lamb

A Division of The McGraw·Hill Companies

Columbus, Ohio

www.sra4kids.com

SRA/McGraw-Hill

*A Division of The **McGraw·Hill** Companies*

Send all inquiries to:
SRA/McGraw-Hill
8787 Orion Place
Columbus, OH 43240-4027

ISBN 0-07-569834-X
   3 4 5 6 7 8 9 DBH 05 04 03 02

I am Lora Lamb.
I am small.
I cannot think, but I am not dumb.

I can do what you can do with
the help of a thumb.

I can grab a limb.

I can pick up crumbs.

I can pet a dog.
I am soft.

I am Lora Lamb.
I am a puppet.